Creatures of the **Forest Habitat**

Bobcats

Caitie McAneney

PowerKiDS press.

New York

Published in 2017 by The Rosen Publishing Group, Inc.
29 East 21st Street, New York, NY 10010

First Edition

Editor: Caitie McAneney
Book Design: Mickey Harmon

Photo Credits: Cover (series logo) iLoveCoffeeDesign/Shutterstock.com; cover, pp. 1, 3, 4, 6, 8, 10, 12, 14, 16, 18, 20, 22—24 (background) BlueRingMedia/Shutterstock.com; cover (bobcat) Dennis W. Donohue/Shutterstock.com; p. 5 Don Fink/Shutterstock.com; p. 7 Michael & Patricia Fogden/Minden Pictures/Getty Images; p. 9 (main) Geoffrey Kuchera/Shutterstock.com; p. 9 (opossum) Lisa Hagan/Shutterstock.com; p. 9 (deer) Tom Worsley/Shutterstock.com; p. 9 (squirrel) colin robert varndell/Shutterstock.com; p. 10 James Hagar/robertharding/Getty Images; p. 11 Ian Duffield/Shutterstock.com; pp. 13, 14, 15 (mountain lion) Debbie Steinhausser/Shutterstock.com; p. 15 (coyote) sebartz/Shutterstock.com; p. 15 (wolf) Seokhee Kim/Shutterstock.com; p. 15 (main) Svetlana Foote/Shutterstock.com; p. 16 (goats) Greenfire/Shutterstock.com; p. 16 (sheep) unverdorben jr/Shutterstock.com; p. 16 (cows) majeczka/Shutterstock.com; p. 17 P. DOTSON/Getty Images; p. 19 Barrett Hedges/Getty Images; p. 21 Holly Kuchera/Shutterstock.com; p. 22 Bildagentur Zoonar GmbH/Shutterstock.com.

Cataloging-In-Publication Data

Names: McAneney, Caitie.
Title: Bobcats / Caitie McAneney.
Description: New York : PowerKids Press, 2017. | Series: Creatures of the forest habitat | Includes index.
Identifiers: ISBN 9781499427103 (pbk.) | ISBN 9781499429305 (library bound) | ISBN 9781499427110 (6 pack)
Subjects: LCSH: Bobcat–Juvenile literature.
Classification: LCC QL737.C23 M367 2017 | DDC 599.75'36–d23

Manufactured in the United States of America

CPSIA Compliance Information: Batch #BW17PK: For Further Information contact Rosen Publishing, New York, New York at 1-800-237-9932

Contents

Stealthy Cats

Bobcats are the most common of all wild cats in the United States, but you'll probably never see one. That's because these big cats are masters of **stealth**. Bobcats like to live in places where it's easy to hide. Their homes include deserts, wetlands, and especially forests.

How did the bobcat get its name? Its tail is shorter than that of most cats. The tail is said to look "bobbed," or cut short. Read on to learn more about this forest cat!

Forest Friend Facts

A bobcat is about twice the size of a large house cat.

Bobcats are usually active at night. That makes them even harder to find!

5

Where Can You Find a Bobcat?

If you live in North America, a bobcat might be living nearby. Bobcats can be found from southern Canada to Mexico and all across the United States. Some have **adapted** to the cold winter weather in Canada. Others survive the hot summers of the southeastern United States and Mexico. Some live in dry deserts, while others live in swamps and marshes such as the Everglades in Florida. People have even found bobcats living in **suburban** areas across the continent.

Forest Friend Facts

Bobcats adapt well to new environments. That helps them survive.

These bobcats sit in a tree in the Chihuahuan Desert in Mexico. They're used to the dry heat.

7

A Forest Habitat

A habitat is an animal's natural home. It has all the things an animal needs, such as food, water, and shelter. What's the perfect home for a cat that likes to hide? A forest!

Forest habitats are full of trees and plants. This makes it easy to hide, especially for bobcats. They're great at climbing trees. Bobcats also like to scratch trees, just like house cats scratch a post. That helps them mark their **territory**.

Forest Friend Facts

Bobcats take shelter in logs and hollow trees, or under rocky ledges.

squirrel

deer

opossum

Other animals of the forest habitat include squirrels, opossums, and deer. These animals better be on the lookout for the bobcat!

9

Bobcat Bodies

Bobcats grow to around 50 inches (127 cm) long. They can be as heavy as 30 pounds (13.6 kg). They are built for running, jumping, and hunting.

Bobcats have big paws and long legs. Their fur is usually brown, tan, or reddish. The spotted pattern on their fur helps bobcats blend in with their surroundings. That's called camouflage. It helps them hide and sneak up on their **prey**. Bobcats have black tips on their ears and tails. Their most famous feature is their short tail.

Forest Friend Facts

Bobcats that live in snowy habitats often have lighter fur to help them blend in with their surroundings.

lynx

Bobcats look a lot like their cat cousin, the lynx. However, the lynx has a tail that's black all around, while the bobcat's tail is black on top and white on the bottom.

Bobcat Babies

Bobcats usually like to live alone. However, they do come together to mate, or make babies. This happens in the winter and early spring.

Female bobcats give birth to a litter of kittens. They may have as few as one kitten or as many as six kittens. Bobcat kittens are born blind and rely on their mother. She feeds them milk and teaches them how to hunt. By the time they're a year old, they're ready to leave their mother and find their own food.

Forest Friend Facts

Bobcats can live nearly 13 years in the wild!

Bobcat kittens can stay safe inside logs like this one.

Bobcats on the Hunt

Bobcats are great hunters. They like to stalk, or silently follow, their prey. They use their great senses of sight and hearing to track the animal. They'll hide behind plants and trees, waiting without a sound. Then, suddenly, they will run and **pounce**. A bobcat can leap up to 10 feet (3 m)!

Bobcats will eat nearly any animal, which makes them **opportunistic** hunters. After a bobcat has killed a large animal, it may cover the body to save for later.

wolf

mountain lion

coyote

Bobcat predators include wolves, mountain lions, and coyotes.

Favorite Foods

Bobcats are able to survive in changing habitats because of their opportunistic diet. They love to eat rabbits, which are found in forests and other habitats across North America. Other small animals such as squirrels and mice are also favorite foods.

Bobcats are able to take down much larger prey, too. They can hunt deer, goats, and sheep. These animals can be bigger than the bobcat itself. Farmers and ranchers blame bobcats for killing **livestock**, such as cows and sheep.

goats

sheep

cows

Bobcats love to eat birds. The cats' ability to pounce comes in handy when hunting them!

17

Bobcats and People

Bobcats usually stay far away from humans. In fact, if a bobcat comes near you, it may be sick with **rabies** or another illness. If you see one, make a lot of noise and back away slowly.

Sometimes bobcats enter neighborhoods. They usually need to be removed from the area if they are a **threat**. Bobcats are more of a threat to pets than to humans. Always keep your pets inside at night to protect them from attacks by wild animals.

Forest Friend Facts

Most mammals can carry rabies, which is one reason why it's important to stay away from wild animals.

Before you go hiking or camping, always do **research** about the wildlife you might run into.

19

Bobcat Threats

Humans are the biggest threat to bobcats. People build houses and farms on land where bobcats live. They take down trees that the bobcats once used for shelter and hiding places. Some people accidentally kill bobcats with their car as the animals are crossing the street.

Some hunters kill bobcats for sport. Other hunters kill bobcats for their fur, or pelt. They catch the bobcats using harmful traps. They sell the pelts for a lot of money. Despite these threats, the **species** is not at risk of dying out. There are more than 1 million bobcats in North America.

You can help keep wild animals safe by never wearing real fur. If people stop buying bobcat fur, hunters may stop killing them.

21

Save the Forest

Forests are sometimes called Earth's lungs. The many trees produce oxygen, which we need to breathe. They're also home to many animals, such as bobcats.

Bobcats are masters of their forest habitat. They are great at stalking and pouncing on their prey. They use trees for shelter and scratching. They can adapt to many different temperatures, and they'll eat all kinds of prey. You may never catch a glimpse of the bobcat in the wild, but this animal is the king of the forest!

Glossary

adapt: To change in order to live better in a certain environment.

environment: Everything that surrounds a living thing.

livestock: Farm animals that are kept, raised, and used by people.

opportunistic: Feeding on whatever food is available.

pounce: To jump suddenly toward or onto something.

prey: An animal hunted by other animals for food.

rabies: A deadly disease that affects the central nervous system. It is carried in the spit of some animals.

research: Studying to find something new.

species: A group of plants or animals that are all the same kind.

stealth: The act of doing something quietly and secretly.

suburban: A town or other area where people live in houses near a larger city.

territory: An area of land that an animal considers to be its own and will fight to defend.

threat: Something likely to cause harm.

Index

Websites

Due to the changing nature of Internet links, PowerKids Press has developed an online list of websites related to the subject of this book. This site is updated regularly. Please use this link to access the list: www.powerkidslinks.com/forest/bobc